The Christ Chaplain
The Way to a Deeper, More Effective Hospital Ministry

THE HAWORTH PASTORAL PRESS®
Haworth Series in Chaplaincy
Andrew J. Weaver, Mth, PhD
Editor

The Christ Chaplain
The Way to a Deeper, More Effective Hospital Ministry

Robert John Pennington
(AKA M. Basil Pennington)

The Haworth Pastoral Press®
An Imprint of The Haworth Press, Inc.
New York

For more information on this book or to order, visit
http://www.haworthpress.com/store/product.asp?sku=5931

or call 1-800-HAWORTH (800-429-6784) in the United States and Canada
or (607) 722-5857 outside the United States and Canada

or contact orders@HaworthPress.com

Published by

The Haworth Pastoral Press®, an imprint of The Haworth Press, Inc., 10 Alice Street, Binghamton, NY 13904-1580.

PUBLISHER'S NOTE
The development, preparation, and publication of this work has been undertaken with great care. However, the Publisher, employees, editors, and agents of The Haworth Press are not responsible for any errors contained herein or for consequences that may ensue from use of materials or information contained in this work. The Haworth Press is committed to the dissemination of ideas and information according to the highest standards of intellectual freedom and the free exchange of ideas. Statements made and opinions expressed in this publication do not necessarily reflect the views of the Publisher, Directors, management, or staff of The Haworth Press, Inc., or an endorsement by them.

Cover design by Kerry E. Mack.

Library of Congress Cataloging-in-Publication Data

Pennington, M. Basil
   The Christ chaplain : the way to a deeper, more effective hospital ministry / Robert John Pennington.
      p. cm.
   Includes bibliographical references and index.
   ISBN: 978-0-7890-0647-9 (case : alk. paper)
   ISBN: 978-0-7890-0901-2 (soft : alk. paper)
      1. Chaplains, Hosptial. 2. Church work with the sick. 3. Contemplation. 4. Prayer—Christianity.
   I. Title.

BV4375.P46 2007
259'.411—dc22
                                                                                    2006035938

To
Hospital Chaplains
who give themselves so generously
to bringing care, consolation, and love
to their sisters and brothers
in Christ.

I was sick and you visited me.

IN MEMORIUM

Fr. M. Basil (Robert) Pennington was born on July 28, 1931. He attended the Minor Seminary of Brooklyn, the Cathedral College of the Immaculate Conception, from 1945 to 1950.

In February 1951 he paid his first visit to St. Joseph's Abbey and was convinced that this was the place he wished to make his home. He entered on June 18, 1951, and after two years of novitiate made his Profession on July 26, 1953. After the completion of priestly studies he was ordained priest on December 21, 1957.

Dom M. Basil (Robert) Pennington, OCSO
July 28, 1931-June 3, 2005

The following year he was chosen to go to Rome for studies. After a scholastic year at the Pontifical University of St. Thomas Aquinas (then known as the "Angelicum") he received a licentiate (roughly equivalent to master's degree) in theology. He returned to Spencer in 1959 where he was appointed professor of theology.

In September 1961 he was once again sent to Rome, this time to study canon law at the Gregorian University. In 1962 he received a baccalaureate and in 1963, a licentiate in canon law, on both occasions with the highest honors. Returning to Spencer, he was appointed professor of canon law and of spirituality. Apart from his teaching commitments he was active in the Law Commission of the Order, of which he was chosen a member in 1967.

In March 1968 at his suggestion a project was discussed for a series of publications that was to include translations of the Cistercian Fathers into English and other studies in the area of Cistercian life and spirituality. In May of the same year plans for "Cistercian Publications" were accepted by the superiors of the American Cistercian monasteries of the Strict Observance at their regional meeting, and in January 1969 a first volume was published.

The following year the First International Cistercian Studies Symposium was held at Spencer. This was destined to be the first of a series of similar meetings that have continued down to the present time. These are currently hosted each year in conjunction with the annual International Medieval Studies Congress at Western Michigan University in Kalamazoo.

During the 1970s Fr. Basil's commitments both within the United States and abroad increased considerably. These included visits to other monasteries around the world for conferences.

His growing interest in the spirituality of Eastern Orthodoxy during the 1970s brought him to Greece and to Mount Athos for an extended visit. This led to the publication of *O Holy Mountain* in 1978, which added to the already impressive list of his published works.

In 1978 he became Vocation Director at Spencer, an important office which he filled for a number of years. In 1981 his travels extended even farther—to India for a seminar on Monasticism in World Religions and for lectures at the Cistercian monasteries in the Philippines and on Lantao Island near Hong Kong.

It was also during the 1970s that he became increasingly interested in centering prayer, which had first been taught at Spencer by Fr. William Meninger. This was to become one of his most cherished interests during the last decades of his life. His frequent sessions and workshops throughout the world in the 1980s and 1990s made a lasting impression upon those who participated in them.

In 1991 he went to assist the monastery of Our Lady of Joy on Lantao Island near Hong Kong. Apart from yearly attendance at the Cistercian Studies Conferences in Kalamazoo, his activities during these years were largely limited to Asia. On July 12, 1999, he returned to the United States, where a new type of work awaited him—on February 14, 2000, he was named temporary superior at Assumption Abbey in Ava, Missouri, an appointment that was to last only a short time, for on August 4 of that year he was elected Abbot of the Cistercian Monastery of the Holy Spirit in Conyers, Georgia.

On May 12, 2002, he resigned this office and returned to his home at Spencer, where he was finally able to find some rest from his many labors, without forgetting, however, all those whose hearts he had touched in his many workshops and days of recollection. Indeed, they would always occupy a special place in his own heart alongside his own Spencer brethren.

Just as the monks were chanting Second Vespers for the Solemnity of the Sacred Heart of Jesus, our Father Basil breathed his last, reposing in the lord on the bright and mild day of June 3, 2005. The feast of God's love and mercy was one of his favorite devotions. So it is consoling that after sustaining the weighty injuries of a very serious car accident sixty-seven days before, he yielded the battle accepting the Lord's welcome into his eternal home on that very special day.

May choirs of angels guide him to that place where he may join the saints in singing "Holy, Holy, Holy!" The community of Spencer monks thanks all who offered prayers for Father Basil during his passion and we ask your continued prayer for the repose of his soul in light and peace. May Jesus Christ, his Lord, come to embrace him for ever. Amen.

CONTENTS

Foreword

Reading *The Christ Chaplain* transported me back to the beginning of my ministry more than thirty years ago. I had newly returned to *Hawai'i*, after completing my studies in Berkeley. I was prepared to assume a parish position in my island church, yet I felt inexplicably drawn away from the fanfare and elation of homecoming to a barren, windswept peninsula, across a rough water channel on a neighboring island of *Moloka'i*, named *Ka-laupapa*, which means "flat plain."

This lone promontory jutting out into a caldron of seething Pacific whitecaps is inaccessible by land except for a switchback trail ascending three miles to the "topside" of the island. A long stretch of black sand beach at the foot of the steep razorback cliffs leads to a small settlement dwarfed by leaning coconut trees. History has illuminated this remote landing seemingly immune from time and memory as the healing refuge of Damien the Leper Priest and his beloved flock.

In the early 1800s Hawaiians infected with the *bacillus leprae* were torn away from their families and banished for life to this desolate plain. For an indigenous people whose cultural identity is defined by belonging to a group, social isolation was even more unbearable than the disease that ravaged only the body. Abandonment and forced exile leeched the soul.

Into this remote outpost of human suffering stepped a young Belgium missionary named Joseph De Veuster in 1873. He came to care for the neglected outcasts who had been civilly banned from society as effectively as in biblical times. With him he

The Christ Chaplain
© 2007 by The Haworth Press, Inc. All rights reserved.
doi:10.1300/5931_a

brought a simple faith and the willingness to accompany lost souls during their final journey.

If, as Abraham Maslow suggested, we can learn what it means to be human by studying the exemplars of our traditions, then certainly Damien captures the complexities and ambiguities of being a chaplain as few others have for me. Somewhere in the mix of his struggle to do ministry and confrontation with his own limitations he discovered a place within that was transformative and life-giving. Now in *The Christ Chaplain,* Fr. Basil guides us to that place.

The Christ Chaplain is written for hospital chaplains who often find themselves at the limits of what they can do and endure in living out their calling. Fr. Basil invites us to enter the Christian mystical tradition via *lectio* and centering prayer. It is a path of learning receptivity and *emptying,* that we may rest in the Source at the heart of our being, and show others the way there too. Contemplative Outreach is an international movement of laypeople committed to the practice of centering prayer.

Unlike many popular volumes for chaplains today, which focus on doing ministry better, differently, or more effectively, Fr. Basil cuts to the heart of the matter by emphasizing not what a chaplain *does* but who the chaplain *is*. His instructions on centering and presence are welcome correctives to the clerical culture's fascination with shortcuts and "how-to" manuals. As one who has spent many years in the continuing formation of clergy and clinical pastoral education, I applaud this emphasis.

While Fr. Basil does present a tried-and-true method for centering, he offers it as the proverbial raft that helps us to the other side of the river. The destination is resting in God's presence at the core of our being; centering is simply the means to that end.

Fr. Basil introduced me to centering prayer more than twenty years ago at a Mastery seminar in Boston where a small group of like-minded religious gathered to consider the possibility of transformational ministry. I remember his drawing fire from ecclesiastical authorities for what was then considered controversial methods and approaches. But he stood unwavering in his openness to the new and developed an international network of support for people like myself, religious and clergy, young and old, who came to him seeking not only "new wine" for their ministries but "new wineskins" as well.

What moves me about Fr. Basil is the largeness and largess of his Cistercian heart for those in pastoral ministry. His voluminous writings on prayer and spirituality, where *The Christ Chaplain* now assumes its place, are a record of his generous commitment to share the riches of monastic prayer with those in ministry. This book is a small gem that I recommend to be read as when on a retreat, prayerfully and receptively.

I found *The Christ Chaplain* brought me full circle to my work today as a hospice chaplain by evoking memories of Damien and my initiation into ministry. Fr. Basil knows well the inner geography Damien walked. He shares with us the path to the silent Presence that is in our heart of hearts. Likewise, we also may learn that it is entering the heart of disease, suffering, and progressive debilitation, that we can discover unexpected gifts of grace, presence, and joy.

Clarence Liu
Hospice Hawaii
September 2003

Introduction

Andrew J. Weaver

[Contemplation] is a country whose center is everywhere and whose circumstance is nowhere. You do not find it by traveling but by standing still.

Thomas Merton
Seeds of Contemplation

There are 353,000 Christian and Jewish clergy serving congregations in the United States (4,000 rabbis; 49,000 Catholic priests; and 300,000 Protestant ministers, according to the U.S. Department of Labor, 1998). In addition, there are 92,107 sisters and 6,578 brothers in Catholic religious orders nationwide (Stark & Finke, 2000) and more than 10,000 chaplains working in health care institutions (VandeCreek & Burton, 2001). These are among the most trusted and hard-working professionals in our society (Gallup & Lindsay, 1999).

In a national survey of almost 2,000 United Methodist pastors, Professor Dennis Orthner at the University of North Carolina found that their work can be rewarding, but that it is highly demanding. On average, United Methodist clergypersons spend 56.2 hours per week in ministry and twelve evenings a month away from home on church duties (Orthner, 1986). About one in four of the surveyed pastors work more than sixty hours a week. In addition, although clergy rank in the top 10 percent of the population in terms of education, they rank 325 out of 432 occupations in terms

The Christ Chaplain
© 2007 by The Haworth Press, Inc. All rights reserved.
doi:10.1300/5931_01

of salaries received (Morris & Blanton, 1995). In part because of time pressures and financial distress, unfortunately the burnout syndrome has increasingly become associated with pastoral work.

Health care chaplains are often under the added high stress that has become endemic in modern medicine. Economic pressures are impacting all health care professionals, resulting in less time spent with patients. Hospital staff, to whom chaplains minister, work under increasing stress as a result of the sophisticated demands of modern technology. Experts emphasize the importance of adequate self-care on the part of health care professionals, including chaplains. Making a priority of one's spiritual health is essential to ensure effective ministry.

The Christ Chaplain: The Way to a Deeper, More Effective Hospital Ministry by Father M. Basil Pennington, is a valuable, instructive book that can help chaplains and other religious professionals seeking better spiritual health. The book is about how one can be more effective as a health care chaplain through practicing spiritual self-care in a form of contemplative prayer. Centering prayer is a method of contemplative prayer in which a person pays attention to God dwelling in the center of his or her being. This type of praying is rooted in silence. It is a receptive mode of prayer that seeks a personal relationship with God. It is like two friends sitting in silence, just being in each other's presence. Centering prayer is drawn from the ancient prayer practices of the Christian contemplative heritage, notably the Fathers and Mothers of the Desert, The Cloud of Unknowing, St. John of the Cross, St. Teresa of Avilla, and *lectio divina* (praying the scriptures).

Lectio divina means literally the divine reading. It is a monastic term for the meditative reading of the scriptures. Its elements are the ingredients to a spiritual frame of mind, a discipline of dwelling on a biblical text as the means of seeking communion with Christ. *Lectio divina* has four elements: (1) *lectio* itself, which means reading, understood as the careful repetitious recitation of a short text of scripture; (2) *meditatio* or meditation, an effort to fathom the meaning of the text and make it personally relevant to oneself in Christ; (3) *oratio,* which means prayer, taken as a personal response to the text, asking for the grace of the text or moving over it toward union with God; and (4) *contemplatio,* translated contemplation, gazing at length on something. The idea behind this final element is that by the infused grace of God, one is raised above meditation to a state of seeing or experiencing the text as mystery and reality. It is an exposure to the divine presence, truth, and compassion.

Similar to his friend Thomas Merton, Father Pennington has devoted his life to learning how to pray well. Merton and Pennington have found that contemplation can bring a sense of oneness that we can feel with life itself, with other people, and with God. These are moments when we experience a fuller peace and harmony. Such moments can help renew our souls when ministry is draining our spirit. Thomas Merton speaks to us of the joy that can bring renewal of the spirit through prayer and contemplation. In his book *Seeds of Contemplation* he writes, "The only true joy is to escape from the prison of our own selfhood . . . and enter by love into union with the Life Who dwells and sings within the essence of every creature and in the core of our minds."

May *The Christ Chaplain* bring you joy and song.

REFERENCES

Gallup, G.H., & Lindsay, D.M. (1999). *Surveying the religious landscape: Trends in U.S. beliefs.* Harrisburg, PA: Morehouse Publishing.

Morris, M.L., & Blanton, P.W. (1995). The availability and importance of denominational support services as perceived by clergy husbands and wives. *Pastoral Psychology, 44(1),* 29-44.

Orthner, D.K. (1986). *Pastoral counseling: Caring and caregivers in the United Methodist Church.* Nashville, TN: The General Board of Higher Education and Ministry of The United Methodist Church.

Stark, R., & Finke, R. (2000). *Acts of Faith: Explaining the human side of religion.* Berkeley, CA: University of California Press.

United States Department of Labor. (1998). *Occupational Outlook Handbook.* Washington, DC: Bureau of Labor Statistics.

VandeCreek, L., & Burton, L. (2001). Professional chaplaincy: Its role andimportance in healthcare. *Journal of Pastoral Care, 55(1),* 81-97.

Chapter 1

Welcome

The image is as vivid in my mind's eye as it was fifty years ago: the long rows of beds in the drab green ward. It was the women's ward for MS (multiple sclerosis) patients in King's County Hospital. Each Saturday I would make my way along the line, visiting these women, many of them much too young, trapped in bodies that no longer responded to their least desires. I searched for words of comfort and consolation, for words that might give them some hope as they faced the empty years that lay ahead. By the end of the afternoon I was drained. I felt like some giant hand had roughly wrung me out.

I am sure that for most hospital chaplains the situation is quite different today. But I am sure we all share that pain and frustration when confronted with exposed human misery and we have not the salve to at least alleviate some of its burning. As the day wears on, and there are days after days, we ourselves begin to feel very raw. How much more can we take? Can our empathy stretch to cover yet another wound? In the freshness of the morning when we rise from our prayer, that which we want so much to bring to our dear patients that day seems in the succeeding hours to be wholly consumed. There seems to be nothing left to give beyond the worn-out words and the sacramental signs. How can we tap into the bottomless wells of the divine compassion? How can we somehow be the sacrament of the radiant hope of the risen Lord? How can we ourselves be saved from discouragement and despair, or just from that

The Christ Chaplain
© 2007 by The Haworth Press, Inc. All rights reserved.
doi:10.1300/5931_02

5

brownout that hardly brings comfort and light into the room and the heart of the sufferer? We need to know the way to the Source, how to get in touch with the Source, at least on a daily basis, but also how to step aside and dip in when we begin to realize we are close to drained. There is an old saying: It is better to teach a man how to fish than to give him fish. But maybe he needs a fish right now, before he can begin to learn. We need to bring Christ, with his strengthening comfort and consolation, to each one we are privileged to serve. It would be well if we can also put our patients in touch with the Source, show them the way to the Source, so that they themselves, as much as they want and need, can draw from the Living Water.

In many hospitals today, the patients fall largely into one of two categories: the quick in and out and the one who has come there to die. The former gives the chaplain little opportunity to develop a relationship with the patient. So many of our Lord's encounters were of this quickly passing sort. There comes to my mind immediately the day four young men were determined to see that their friend got to Jesus. They were soon dragging their jerry-rigged stretcher to the roof and pulling off the roof tiles. Jesus appreciated their energetic faith and responded, but in a way that was not quite expected. To the sick man: "Your sins are forgiven you." Challenged, Jesus immediately related the physical sickness to the sickness of the soul. Responding to faith, bringing a healing word to the spirit of our patient, we may be doing far more than anyone expects toward promoting physical healing. Albeit a quickly passing meeting, a word of faith, love, and compassion can make a difference.

Deathbed ministry is at the heart of Christianity. Jesus responded to the plea of his fellow sufferer: "This day you will be with me in paradise." Catholics like to speak of this good thief as the first canonized saint. It takes but a moment, a subtle movement of the soul, to turn around one's life and face the all-merciful and saving Lord. It will probably only be in paradise that we will come to know how many have heard our word or been touched by our presence and found healing and the heavenly gate.

We are, of course, very aware that we are not the only ones ministering to the spiritual welfare of our patients. Doctors and nurses, perhaps more so today than ever before, are concerned about the spiritual well-being of patients and minister to them in many ways. Nonetheless we chaplains have a distinctive ministry. A part of our ministry is to be a manifest sign that God does care, cares enough to send someone to the patient, to come to them in the person of a minister. This demands that we do have a grateful respect for the ministry of doctors and nurses and other members of the hospital team, even while we have a special responsibility in the way we act, the way we speak, the way we try to be Christlike, to be a Christ-presence.

It is obvious then that the key to our ministry is to come as Christ, and there is certainly nothing artificial about this. We have been baptized into Christ. "I live now, not I, but Christ lives in me." We want to realize our Christness more and more and to put on "the mind of Christ." "Let this mind be in you that was in Christ Jesus. . . ." In the pages of this little book we talk about acquiring the mind of Christ, and his heart. And how to help our patients get in touch with this. What we have to say will be simple and practical, but let me assure you, it can be profoundly transforming. I speak out of decades as practitioner and teacher. It is a sure way to come to him and be refreshed, to taste and see how good the Lord is.

This is essentially a book about prayer. I think Sean O'Malley put it well in the course of his homily at his installation mass in Boston:

> Formation in prayer must become the determining point in every pastoral program. In prayer, we shall discover the primacy of grace and discover that without God we can do nothing. In prayer, we will find the strength to carry out the mission entrusted to us to walk in humility and love and prac-

tice mercy with all. St. Ignatius put it so well: "We must pray as if everything depended on God, and work as if everything depended upon us."

It is simple, but not easy. Because it demands that we turn from our self-centeredness to Christ-centeredness. We will only be all we want to be as chaplains and all that our patients want and need when we come as Christ. Our own unique expression of Christ—true. For the Lord loves us and delights in the unique person he has made each one of us.

As you read along you may find that some of the scriptural quotations sound somewhat different to you. I think most modern authors decide what texts they want to use and then turn to some chosen, accepted translation and copy the texts precisely from that translation, which is often acknowledged at the beginning of the volume. I function a bit more like the writers and preachers of the centuries before the printing press. I quote scripture from memory. In editing I can check my translation with the original Greek or Hebrew, though sometimes I prefer to follow the Vulgate or the Vetus Latina. In any case I think most would agree in these days when we have so many fine accepted translations—New Revised Standard Version, New American Bible, New Jerusalem, etc.—that texts can indeed be legitimately translated in different ways and that it can be useful for us to hear different translations. The variety of interpretation invites us to look more deeply into what the text means for us and in our lives, what the Lord is actually saying to us now.

I would like to be able to sit down with you, hear your story, get better acquainted with you and your ministry. That unfortunately is not possible. I have been blessed with sharing the stories of many through the years. They add much to the limited wisdom that comes from my own experience, but I know the little I say here will have to play into your own experience and ministry with its many facets. My prayer is that it may in fact be helpful for you and for all those to whom you bring Christ's love and blessings, his gentle, abiding care and love.

Chapter 2

To Know Him:
Acquiring the Mind of Christ

I ascended very early. I wanted to enjoy the serenity of the
Acropolis before the sun began to burn and the hoards of tourists
began to arrive. Soon enough the large buses put in their appearance and disgorged the eager masses who rushed about with cam-
eras clicking. Before they had an chance to experience the reality
that they were capturing on their celluloid their taskmaster herded
them back aboard their buses to hasten them on to the next bit of
history.

As I looked down from the commanding height of the Acropolis
I could see the nearby Areopagus, the place where the Acts of the
Apostles report that Paul preached to the Athenians. What a different sight. The mount boasted few archeological remains. In that
early morning hour only two figures graced its fairly nude summit.
One walked about in silent meditation; the other sat on a sizeable
rock, a Bible open on her lap. I could not help but sense that they
were seeking not the tourists' novelties but rather Saint Paul's Unknown God.

All those centuries ago the missionary from Tarsus brought to
the Athenians the good news: "The God whom I proclaim is in fact
the one whom you already worship without knowing it—An Unknown God." It is a stretch to worship an Unknown God. It is really impossible to love such a one; no one can love what one does
not know.

The Christ Chaplain
© 2007 by The Haworth Press, Inc. All rights reserved.
doi:10.1300/5931_03

The human heart, the human being, is made for love. Whether we know it or not, and most of us in our better moments know it, this is what we long for: to love and to be loved, to live in the embrace of a mutual love. If in some way we always sense it, even if that sensing comes out of a deprived infancy and youth, we know it even more when the usual distractions of life are stripped away or perhaps slipping away permanently. We walk or hasten down the corridors of a hospital to bring love, with all its hope and peace and promise, to hearts that long for it. The love we bring is, of course, not an "it"—love never is; it is a person. It is the God who is love and who became one of us to calm our fears—how often did he say: "Fear not. It is I"?—to touch our hearts and fulfill all our longings. As Christian chaplains we come to bring Christ, to be the Christ who we are, and as Christ to be present in love.

My old theology teacher, leaning on the smattering of Latin we were reputed to have acquired used to say: *"Nemo dat quod none got!"* ("No one gives what one does not have."). Even though we as women and men baptized into Christ are always possessed by him, can we in turn so possess him in love in a way that will be meaningful and satisfy the longing hearts of our sisters and brothers whom we come to serve if we do not truly know him?

We have all heard many sermons, read many books, perhaps studied much theology. We know a lot *about* him, but that is not enough. The question is: do we know him, truly know him? The devil (and many theologians, too) know a lot more about him than we will ever know. But the devil can never know him nor help others to know him in the way that leads to and satisfies the longings of the human heart, in the way that love alone can reveal him. When we know the Lord in the way of love then we can, indeed, bring him and make him present when we stand beside the one to whom we minister.

How do we come to know the Lord in this way? How do we come to know anyone in this way? By spending time with them in openness, an openness that allows the other to reveal themselves to us.

THE SACRED TEXT

Our God is a revealing God. This is an awesome gift we share with our Jewish sisters and brothers: we are the children of the Book. If you have not personally experienced it, perhaps you have read Cham Potock's *My Name Is Asser Lev.* In the climax of his story he describes it well: the Feast of Simcha Torah: the celebration of the Torah, the gift of revelation. It is always something special when the rabbi takes the sacred scrolls from the ark. As he passes through the congregations, eager hands reach out the touch the sacred burden, to place thereon a kiss of total homage. But on the Feast of Simcha Torah, this is not enough. One after the other, the devoted disciples grasp the sacred burden, hug it to their breasts, and enter an ecstatic dance. It is the union of God and God's beloved, a moment of intimate union—truly a sacrament of communion.

Do we Christians treasure enough what is ours in the inspired Word, in the book we call the Bible? Do we enthrone it in our homes, in our offices? Or do we just drop it on the desk or put it on the shelf with the other books? It is a Presence. God is in his Word. God is there to be to us, to speak to us, to invite us into intimacy: "I no longer call you servants but friends, because I make known to you all that I have heard from the Father."

LECTIO DIVINA

If we explore the first books written in the West about Christian spirituality—and it perdures as long as Latin was the language of the Christian West—we find the authors speaking of "lectio" or at times, *lectio divina.* When I have been forced to employ a translator to lecture to a group whose language I did not know, I have often teased my translator by having this good soul translate an old Latin adage: *Traductor traditor est.* "The translator is a traitor." It is true: every translation betrays the original. It leaves behind so many of the nuances, so much of the depths of meaning of the original only to take on the nuances and deeper meanings of the new word. "Lectio" literally means "reading"—*lectio divina,* divine reading. But such a translation certainly sells short if not totally betrays the meaning of the original. Indeed, in that early Christian period most of the people could not read. Of those who could read, relatively few would be rich enough to own a book or manuscript, much less a whole Bible. Only the most wealthy or an institution would have such a treasure, the labor of many months, the hide of flocks of sheep.

Lectio rather means "receiving"—receiving with an open ear, an open mind, an open heart. Receiving the Word, whether by actually reading, or listening to another read, or reciting a known text, or listening again to the Word written in one's own memory. It involves an awareness that the revealing Word is here and now spoken to me. In coming to lectio, we come into Presence. We perceive in faith that the Lord is indeed present in his Word. God comes to us now in the Word, to speak to us. The Word is a messenger and more than a messenger. It is a sacrament, the outward sign of an inner reality. It makes the inner reality present in a way that the Divine can here and now directly communicate with me. "Speak, Lord, your servant wants to hear."

We come to this encounter we call lectio with an openness—as complete an openness as possible. There comes to my mind a Gospel scene. We are in the hill country, in that hick town called Nazareth—"Can anything good come out of Nazareth?" We find a young woman; we would perhaps think of her as still a girl. Her name is Miriam; we call her Mary. What she is about at this moment is not important. Nothing important ever happens in Nazareth, except perhaps going to the synagogue. The one thing these people know, and they are proud of it, is: There is one God, and that God is our God. On this particular day suddenly an angel puts in an appearance. Mary's people were rather used to angels, so the visit might not have been as startling for her as it would be for one of us. Nonetheless the angel did have to reassure her. The message was the startling thing: Yahweh, their God, has a son. If that was not enough, shattering all the parameters of this young woman's sure knowledge, there comes the even more mind-blowing revelation: Yahweh wants you to be the mother of that son. By the overshadowing of Holy Spirit, the little lady was able to open to and embrace this awesome revelation, sufficiently to be able to make a responsible response: "Be it done unto me according to your word."

This is the attitude we want to bring to our encounter with the living God in our lectio. We want to come into Presence, knowing that God is here in his Word and is speaking to us. We want in openness to be able to let go of all the parameters of our present knowledge and the security we seek in hanging on to them. And with a great dependence on Holy Spirit, who inspired the sacred writers and who now dwells in us, as Jesus promised, to teach us all things and to bring to mind all that he has taught us, we listen, ready to say our "yes" — "Be it done unto me."

We come into presence and call upon Holy Spirit. And then we listen. We listen for a meaningful amount of time. Enough time for us to really hear what the Lord has to say, and perhaps to respond and even talk it over with him. This can, in fact, be a minute or two or three, but in practice we will probably want at least five or ten minutes, if not more. The important thing is that this is a real encounter. We do not want to aim at getting through a certain amount of text, be it the Gospel text of the day's liturgy, a paragraph, or a page. It can then so easily become a task to be done, not a personal meeting. We meet the Lord in the text. He speaks to us. We listen with openness: "Speak, Lord, your servant, your friend wants to hear." And then we let the conversation, the meeting, the encounter move from there. Some days it might well seem just like a lot of words, words we have heard before. We continue to listen. Other days, the very first word, perhaps a very familiar word, will convey a whole world of meaning, a meaning that might take us beyond this world or into its very heart. Or maybe even into the depths of our own heart.

It is quite evident how important the first step in lectio is to the second. We can hardly have a very real sense of listening if we do not sense a speaker present. With a deep sense that the Lord is present in his Word and is here and now ready to speak to me where I am here and now, I will very quickly come to appreciate the importance of calling upon Holy Spirit to help. Even when the Word of the Lord is in itself quite clear, it is not always clear how it applies to my life right now, why the Lord is saying this to me now.

AN EXAMPLE

Take a moment to look at an example.

> One day Jesus summoned the Twelve and began to send them out two by two. He gave them authority over unclean spirits. He instructed them to take nothing for the journey but a walking stick—no food, no sack, no money in their belts. They were, however, to wear sandals but not a second tunic. He said to them, "Wherever you enter a house, stay in that house until you leave from that area. Whatever place does not welcome you or listen to you, leave there and shake the dust off your feet in testimony against them."
>
> So they went off and preached repentance. They drove out many demons. And they anointed with oil many who were sick and cured them.

What is the Lord saying to me here?

"He sent them. . . ." Yes, Lord, it is you who send me down the corridors and into the sickrooms. It is the only reason I am going there. And you send me with the same healing mission, to bring your presence, your word, your hope, your care, your love.

"Do not take anything with you. . . ." I do not need to have years of experience, a degree in psychology or pastoral theology, a certificate in spiritual direction. If I have them, fine. But when I go into that room, it is not to taut what I have. I must go in as a poor one, ready to accept whatever hospitality is offered me.

"If people refuse to listen to you. . . ." You don't demand success. Mine is to bring the Good News. You profoundly respect us all, our freedom. So must I. Each one I approach is free to welcome me or not. It is there freedom. I bring the gift, gently offer it, leave it with them.

"As you walk away, shake off the dust. . . ." If I have received hostility, vituperation, cold indifference, I do not want to let the negative feelings cling to me. As I leave the room, I am to shake off the dust. I am to shake off the negativity so I can go on to the next room free to smile and bring your love.

I might be tempted to see a challenge in the "hard case" and want to expend a lot of time and effort to "crack" it, to break through the shell of indifference or rejection, rather than moving on to more fertile ground where a welcome awaits the good Word or where there is a more urgent need. I need to accept the fact that I cannot reach everyone. You didn't. You do not expect those you send to always succeed.

I am ready to go on to the third step: choose a word. Perhaps one of these words has really spoken loud to me, making me profoundly aware of my need to hear it. Or perhaps no one stands out. I must choose. I choose: "Shake the dust off. . . ." I carry that word with me through the day, repeating it, shaking off each negative thought or feeling or experience I encounter. A whole new attitude begins to develop in me, one that takes a certain amount of the stress out of my life and gives me a new freedom to bring love and life.

THE THIRD STEP

Whether our time is set or flexible the time will come when we have to move on to other responsibilities. (I think it is good for us to have a plan to meet the Lord each day for at least a very short time, two minutes or something that we can certainly fit into every day, but with the sense that most of the time we will freely prolong the meeting according to our possibilities.) Let us be generous enough to say a "thank-you." It is remarkable, is it not? We usually have to go chasing after others to get some of their time. If it is an important person—supervisor, bishop, mayor—we usually have to get an appointment. If we want to speak with the pope we will certainly have to pull some strings. But here is God ready to speak with us whenever we want. All we have to do is open our Bible and listen.

But before we part company, so to speak, let us choose a word, a sentence, a phrase, that God has spoken to us to take with us. In the course of our daily encounter something may have spoken to us with power. We do not need to choose anything; it has been given to us. However, this will not always be our blessing, so we must choose. Carrying a *word* (classically this can mean a word or phrase or short sentence) with us, letting it repeat itself in our mind or heart or even on our lips, was what was commonly meant by the word *meditation* in the course of the first millennium of Christianity. A later scholastic influence changed meditation into a discursive labor. The word we take with us invites the Presence to accompany us as we move on; it invites the Presence to speak to us further through the word in the evolving circumstances of the day. Sometimes when nothing seems to speak to us during the time of our lectio and we choose a word to carry with us through the day, later in the day that word opens and become exceedingly meaningful to us. And sometimes it proves to be just the word that feeds a sister or brother to whom we find ourselves ministering.

ANOTHER EXAMPLE

Let me share with you an experience (one of many) that I have had. On this particular day I met the Lord in lectio early in the morning as is my wont. But he did not seem to show up. I was listening to my most favored passage, the Last Supper discourse. (When we meet the Lord in lectio we can be quite free in choosing the "place": Some like to listen with the Church, using the passage assigned in the lectionary for the daily liturgy; others prefer to read a Gospel straight through, a bit each day; others like to open the Bible randomly and see what the Lord has to say; and sometimes we like to go back to one of our favorite passages, a passage that has already said a lot to us.) On this particular morning as I listened, it all seemed like just so many words: words, words, and more words, words I had heard often before. When it came time to complete my lectio and move on, I choose the Lord's word: "I am the way." A few hours later I was walking down the road to the guesthouse. My word was with me: "I am the way." Suddenly I realized that I was not just walking down a road. I was walking in "the way." I am walking in Christ, who is the Way. I was in the way to fullness of life, eternal life. Since that time, whenever I am walking down a road, a sidewalk, a corridor, a path, I realize that I am walking in "the way." My chosen word that day really came alive and spoke to me in an unforgettable and transforming way.

When I arrived at the guesthouse a young man was waiting to see me. As he poured out his heart I heard just about everything that is in the book and some things that never made the book. I silently prayed: "Lord, what am I going to say to this lad?" Then the Lord sort of poked me in the ribs. Oh yes, I knew. When I shared with the lad the word that I had chosen to walk with me that day, I could see, as it were, the burdens fall from his shoulders. He now had a "way" to go. That day's word was meant not only for me but also for that young man.

The day went on, and it was one of those days. Toward the end of the day I found myself climbing the long flight of stairs that lead up to the abbey church. I was exhausted. And I complained to the Lord: "Lord, how am I ever going to get through evening song? I will sing every note flat!" Once again the Lord, as it were, poked me. "Oh yes, you are the way." So we sang vespers together and it was a good, refreshing experience.

We might sum up this ancient Christian practice of lectio this way:

1. We take the sacred text with reverence and call upon Holy Spirit.
2. For five minutes (longer, if we are so drawn) we listen to the Lord speaking to us through the text and respond.
3. At the end of our time, we choose a word or phrase (perhaps one will have been "given" to us) to take with us and we thank the Lord for being with us and speaking to us.

More briefly we might put it this way:

- Come into the Presence and call upon Holy Spirit.
- Listen for five minutes.
- Thank the Lord and take a "word."

If we each day spend some meaningful time like this with our divine Friend and then share our day with him by means of our chosen word, we will surely come to a deeper, ever more satisfying sense of our Friend. We will come to know him more and more. We will come to have the mind and heart of Christ. We will see things as he sees them, feel as he feels. We will come to be truly a Christ-person.

SCHOOL OF LOVE

Life is essentially a school of love, a way for us to learn to truly give ourselves in love, a journey into the fullness of love. The Master of the school is indeed our God of Love, for as Saint John reminds us, "God is love." God's totally gratuitous outpouring of self, of life and of love, God's constant loving providential care, God's total respect for us, our dignity, our freedom—this our model. To become more accessible to us, God, in a humility that is beyond comprehension, emptied himself and became one with us in Christ Jesus. Jesus, who calls us friends, gives the ultimate example of love: "Greater love than this no one has than that one lay down one's life for one's friends." When we go to the Scriptures and enter our lectio, we sit at the feet of the Master of the school of love. We learn the lessons of self-giving love. When we see things clearly this way, very readily do we admit: there is always more to learn. We need to be constantly encouraged in our practice of the lessons we are learning. We need to be inspired to give ourselves more completely and generously to this school of love, to live love as we go about our daily ministry and all our doings.

John tells us that on one occasion, on the last and greatest day of the feast, Jesus stood up and cried out, "If anyone thirst, let that one come to me and drink. The one who believes in me, as the Scriptures say: 'Out of that one's heart shall flow rivers of living water.'" John goes on to tell us that Jesus said this "about the Spirit, which those who believed in him were to receive." If we regularly meet the Lord in his living Word, there will indeed flow out of our hearts the living Word, the living Spirit, a water of life and comfort for those to whom we minister.

Chapter 3

And His Heart

Let's just pause for a moment. Recall one of the times you entered a relation of love: the first time, the last time, the most important love affair of your life. Or perhaps just imagine one for yourself.

How did it begin? How did you meet? How did you "break the ice"? What were the "getting aquainted" times like? What were the questions you asked? What did you want to know? At first there was a lot of talking, little revelations, things to be shared, stories to be told. You began to seek each other out, find things to do together. So much more was revealed as you experienced things together: how each thought about things, felt, reacted; likes and dislikes, feelings and emotions, style and awkwardness, fear and daring, care and carelessness; what were the shared values. A lot was to be said about all this. The sharings went deeper, became more personal and intimate. But as time went on so much talking began to be just too much. Words were not enough. They just didn't say it. It was time just to be together. That was enough, the union and communion. Our love relationship with God grows in much the same way. In fact, God became one with us in our humanity in order to facilitate this.

As I mentioned in the previous chapter, in our living Christian tradition the word *lectio* means much more than simply reading. In fact it has a very rich and complex meaning. When Saint Benedict wrote his *Rule for Monasteries* he provided at least two hours a

The Christ Chaplain
© 2007 by The Haworth Press, Inc. All rights reserved.
doi:10.1300/5931_04

day and a good bit more some days, especially Sundays and feasts, for lectio. However, he did not expect his men to spend all those hours poring over the Scriptures. For him and for all the early tradition, lectio implied a whole process. It could be summed up in four words: *lectio, meditatio, oratio,* and *contemplatio*—reading, meditation, prayer, and contemplation. It is in the sacred Scriptures that we meet the Lord, get acquainted with him, get to know him (lectio). Little by little our many questions about him begin to be answered. Then with the "word" we take with us from our lectio, we invite the Lord to walk with us (meditation). We begin to get his insights on things, how he sees them, values them, the way he looks at people and the events of life. We no longer need to be alone. We can always have this friend with us, someone with whom we can share everything. We begin to talk to him about things (prayer): Lord, help that dear woman. Lord, what do you think about that? Lord, what should I do here? Lord, help me to find the right words. You know the way; you know the truth; you are the way to truth and life. Prayer begins to seed itself through our whole day. We begin to understand what our Lord was talking about when he urged us to pray constantly, to pray without ceasing. At times when we have had enough of talking, we just want to rest, to be with the Lord (contemplation).

We hear his gentle invitation: Come to me, all you who labor and are heavily burdened, and I will refresh you. We certainly labor, hurrying up and down long corridors, meeting people here and there, standing at bedsides. About the only time we get to sit down is when we open our hearts to be a refuge for the burdens that others need to unload. We labor and are heavily burdened. We need to be refreshed if we are going to be able to continue, day after day, to be there for people, the sick and the well, the fearful, the suffering, the dying, and the many who love them and care for them and share their burdens.

But when we do come to the Lord and seek that refreshment, what happens? We do carve out a bit of time, find a quiet corner.

We do believe he is truly present with us. Did he not say: "The Father and I will come and make our home in you." "I will be with, until the end of time." He is here, but where are we? Our poor, tired mind rushes on. A million thoughts and cares and concerns make themselves felt. Memories rise up from long ago and just now. Feelings and emotions roll through us like so many waves of a sometimes very turbulent ocean. Some days even our nerves seem to be jumping and twitching, giving not even our bodies a chance rest. What are we to do?

Our tradition gives us a little method, a practice to handle all this. Benedict of Nursia, who wrote his *Rule for Monasteries* back in the sixth century, knew it. He sent his men back to an earlier writer, John Cassian, who had learned it when he was a young man from one of the oldest fathers of the desert, Abba Isaac. Later, just as English was emerging as a distinct language, a great spiritual father wrote a treatise about it, *The Cloud of Unknowing*. He expressed it this way: "Choose a word, a simple word. A single-syllable word is best, like 'God' or 'love,' but chose a word that is meaningful to you. Then fix it there, come what may." We take a little word of love. It is a symbol of our intention to consent to God's presence and action within us, to be a complete "yes" to God. And very very gently we let this little word repeat itself within. Whenever, during the time of our resting in the Lord, we find our selves caught up by some other thought, or memory, or feeling, or the like, we very gently return to our little word of love; we return by means of the word to our God of love. We let him hold us close, refresh us, renew us. (Most folks find it is good to take about twenty minutes for the rest—not too long so we can fit it in a very full day but long enough to give us some real rest.)

It is very simple. But anyone who has practiced this way of prayer regularly for a time can tell you how effective it is. I quote from a note one hospital chaplain gave to the administrator of her hospital:

When you write to Basil Pennington, please tell him that centering prayer came at a crucial time in my life and is what has enabled me to stay alive in hospital ministry. Next month, I celebrate my fifteenth year as a chaplain. Several years ago, I found myself exhausted in mind, body, and spirit. I started to "center" in prayer after reading a book by Father Basil and seeing some audiotapes by Thomas Keating. Although I am not always as disciplined as I want to be, I have found such a deep nourishment from practicing centering prayer. Thank you for the ways your centering practice has inspired me to "keep on keeping on."

At first centering prayer can seem difficult. We are so used to paying attention to our own thoughts and feelings. To just let them go is not so easy. We may seem to be losing ourselves, or losing something valuable. But really useful thoughts will come back later, when we need them and can use them. For now we want and need the rest. We need the Lord and his refreshing love. It is simple and it is important to keep it simple: Just sit down, close the eyes gently, turn to the Lord within, tell him of your love and that these twenty minutes are all his, and then begin your little word. It is as simple as that.

It is important for us to be gentle with ourselves. Nothing needs to be accomplished or mastered here. For us, it is just to rest. And no matter how many thoughts or feelings or memories arise, we just gently return to our word as soon as we become aware of our wondering mind. It is not a time for attention, attending to something, setting our attention on something or someone; it is rather a prayer of intention, tending within, resting in the loving embrace of our God of love who dwells within. This prayer has often been called the Prayer of the Heart. The reference, of course, is not to our cardiac organ, but in the biblical sense, to that deepest place within, where God dwells, at every moment bringing us forth in his creative love. Most recently it has acquired the popular name of centering prayer, which perhaps better expresses the reality. We center ourselves upon God who is at the center of our being.

I must confess I have added a little something to the tradition—after all, tradition is a handing on, and every hand makes its imprint. At the end of the time we have set aside for our resting in the Lord—you will recall that I mentioned that most folks find twenty minutes a good amount of time for this prayer; the important thing is to determine the amount of time it is good for you to pray and to be faithful to it—at the end of your time I suggest you let go of your prayer word and allow the prayer the Lord has taught us, the "Our Father," to quietly, gently, and spaciously pray itself within. During our centering prayer we can go very deep. It is good to come out gently. And I have found that when using these words of the Lord at this time, he often gives me insights, which I would have let go if they arose during the time of centering but which I now carry with me back into my active life. Of course, you can freely use any other prayer you might like, or just abide in silence for a bit. The important thing is to come out of the time of contemplation gently.

We can sum up this way of contemplative prayer in this way:

CENTERING PRAYER

Sit relaxed and quiet.

1. Be in faith and love to God who dwells in the center of your being.
2. Take up a love word and let it be gently present, supporting your being to God in faith-filled love.
3. Whenever you become aware of anything, simply, gently return to the Lord with the use of your prayer word.

After twenty minutes let the Our Father (or some other prayer) pray itself.

A FRUITFUL PRAYER

Even though during the time of the prayer we do not attend to any thoughts or feelings or images, we do nonetheless at a level deeper than our attention have an experience of love that opens out in our being a love knowledge, which begins to inform the whole of our life. This is what Saint Paul calls a fruit of the spirit, and it brings with it those other fruits of the spirit: joy, peace, patience, benignity, long-suffering, kindness. Our Lord has told us that it is by the fruit that we are to judge. We will know the fruitfulness of our restful prayer as these grow in our lives. The prayer itself may seem like a void, little more than sleep, or a constant returning from a buzzing of thoughts of all sorts. But each returning is a choice for God, a pure act of love.

It is this love knowledge, in the setting of all the other fruits, that is going to most profoundly affect our ministry. It will give us a certain sureness, a depth of compassion and communion, which will embrace our patients and their loved ones and make a difference. Instead of being caught up in the climate of tension and feverishness, we will be able to bring a restful serenity to our encounters, even when all about us are rushing in intense activity. We will be an oasis of peace, a source of hope, a sign of confidence. We will be Christ, the God of love, in the midst.

If we find it difficult to sit quietly with the Lord for twenty minutes when we want to, letting everything else go—and to be honest, most do—it is a good sign of just how much we need meditation. If our thoughts and feelings, hopes and fears have such a hold on us that we are not free to do what we want to do for twenty minutes, we have really lost something of our humanity. We have been gifted with choice. Yet we all know how we can become so wound up that it seems almost impossible to sit still or we become so obsessed with a project or some fear or some hope or some person we cannot extricate ourselves from a web of thoughts and leave them be while we rest in the divine embrace. This is, of course, why we need a "method," a way to gently free ourselves. With the gentle repetitions of our word we learn to let things go, to ease and quiet the body and the spirit not be paying attention to them but by the gentle movement of love to our Beloved. "Come to me, and I will refresh you." Centering prayer is a way of reestablishing our true freedom as humans, of refinding our true mastery.

Chapter 4

The Ministry of Presence

Within the precincts of our abbey there is a small cottage, the home of the former owner of the property. He had built it himself, with stones and wood from the property itself. It is delightfully designed, with a vaulted, open-beamed living room dominated by a large, effective fireplace, rooms on various levels, a flagstone kitchen, and a small underground chapel. When the monks first arrived it was used as the abbot's quarters. When the new abbey provided the abbot with ample accommodations, the cottage provided a congenial place for the young men coming to explore the monastic life, seeking to see how the monks lived within the cloister.

As there were not always that many seekers to fill all the rooms, I used to welcome other retreatants to the cottage. On one occasion my guest was a very special young priest. He was well known for the virtue of hospitality. He had a wonderful way of being a wide-open, accommodating space for everyone who came along. It was not long after his ordination that he was given a couple of the more difficult ministries in the diocese: the ministry for the divorced and for the gays. Within a few years he was asked to be the spiritual father of the seminarians of the diocese. As his reputation spread he was called to a similar post at the North American College in Rome, where many of the future bishops of the United States are prepared for ordination.

In the course of his visit, I asked Jim how it was that he became such a quiet, welcoming, listening presence, a person with whom

The Christ Chaplain
© 2007 by The Haworth Press, Inc. All rights reserved.
doi:10.1300/5931_05

everyone seemed to immediately feel comfortable and free to share their inmost thoughts and feelings. Jim told me that it came as a gift and he shared his story: He had been ordained just two weeks and arrived at his first assignment a few days earlier. It was a Tuesday and he was "on duty" for the first time. As the quiet evening spent itself, he received a call around ten. It was from the hospital. There had been an auto accident. A parishioner was involved. When he arrived at the hospital he found a really tragic scene: four teenagers, all dead on arrival. The emergency room was chaotic—medical personnel of all descriptions rushing in all directions, new cases being wheeled in, waiting patients and those waiting for them and numerous police officers. All seemed to know just what they were supposed to be doing and doing it very efficiently—all but Jim. He was lost in the turmoil and feeling very lost, completely unknowledgeable and totally inefficient. Suddenly there was a great deal of commotion at the entrance. The families of two of the victims were arriving. The police chief grabbed Jim's arm: "That's your job, Father."

A couple of policemen rather officiously herded the families into a small side room, and sort of pushed Jim in after them. A very distraught and vociferous father loudly demanded: "I want to see my son! Why can't I see my son?" He seemed almost to devour the rather slight priest with his menacing presence. "Why can't I see my son?" Without quite realizing what he was saying, Jim blurted out, "Because he is dead." The stunned families were shocked into silence. They collapsed onto the couch and chairs and some began to sob and even wail. Again, Jim was at a total loss, his heart was completely torn open with their overwhelming loss and grief, so he just sat down and wept with them.

That night when he did finally reach his bed, he tossed and turned. He felt he was a total and complete failure. He couldn't find a word for these poor people. He didn't even break the horrible news with some sort of comforting and uplifting word. All he did was weep, mingling his tears with theirs. Some comfort!

The next day Jim received a phone call from the funeral director in the neighboring town. Although it was outside his parish, the director told him that the parents had asked if Jim might come to lead the vigil service the next evening. Jim was more than happy to be able to provide some service. He could use the ritual, so he would have the words he felt he needed.

As he arrived at the funeral home and eased his way through the immense crowd he became aware that people were noticing him. In fact they seemed to be taking particular notice, pointing him out and making comments to their neighbors. Jim felt sick. Everyone knew what a complete failure he had been, how he had bluntly broke the news, how had had failed to comfort. He led the vigil service as best he could, but again as he looked at the body of this particular young man and sensed the devastating sorrow of his parents, hot tears escaped his eyes and ran down his cheeks. He hardly noticed them and prayed as best he could.

With the service ended, he only managed a warm handshake with each of the parents and then made his way out, accompanied by the funeral director and the boy's uncle. As they emerged into the street the uncle spoke up: "Father, we know you are not from this parish, but the parents would like you to conduct the funeral tomorrow. They have told everyone how wonderful you were the night their son died, how you did not try to fill the air with a lot of pious words but simply sat and wept with them. They know you are truly and fully with them in their grief."

There is a beautiful word: *compassion*. It comes from the Latin: *cum* and *passio,* to feel with. I think this is at the very heart of our ministry, in fact, its very soul. This is the almost unbelievable essence of our Christian faith: our God is a God of compassion. Our God not only feels for us, God feels with us. Our God took on a human body, a human mind, a human heart, human emotions, so that he could feel with us, so that he could feel in his own body, his own heart, his own psyche all that we feel. When we come to the sick, the suffering, the grieving, and all the loved ones who share their pain and grief, we come as Christ—as a Christ chaplain—only if we come with compassion.

This is not easy. For we are not only called upon to be there in sorrow and pain but also in joy and wonderment—when an operation has been a success, when one is released, when parents rejoice in new life. These can be moments of significant ministry, seemingly not so needed but perhaps much more far-reaching in their effect. It is certainly one of the great challenges of our ministry to be able to move from sorrow to joy to sorrow again. It can also be a great challenge to move from the profound to the trivial and to be able to be truly with even the trivial when it is called for. Behind them all is a person, a person loved beyond anything we can imagine by a God who is love. And it is of that love that we, as Christ, are to be sacraments. How few really know God's love as a gentle, tender, caring love, eager to be with us in our joys as well as our sorrows. As Christ chaplains we are to make that love experientially present.

There is a time and place for words. There is an art—and it is truly an art, acquired only with time and experience—to finding the words that authentically express our true compassion, no matter what we have to express. But there are also times, as with Jim's learning experience, when words—any word—would trivialize and be unworthy of such grief. There is a need for the word of faith and hope. That is an important part of our ministry. But there are times when that word cannot be a spoken word. Rather it must be the word that we are, just as Christ is the Word of God. In any case and truly in every case, a word of faith and hope will be heard only if it is spoken out of compassion. And the more fully that compassion is present and experienced the more powerfully the word of faith begets hope.

Where does compassion come from, that kind of compassion that begets faith and hope, that can lift one beyond anything this world has to offer, when this world no longer has anything to offer? This is beyond even the deepest human sentiment, but totally incorporates it. This is the compassion that comes from having the mind and heart of the man who is also God, from having the mind and heart of Christ. Through lectio, thorough complete openness to the revealing Scriptures and the teaching Spirit, we allow the mind of Christ to be formed in us. The heart of Christ, which is a totally human heart, yet the heart of God, the delicate touch that forms and shapes us to feel as Christ feels is crafted within us as we sit in silence with the Beloved and let silence do its work. Lectio and contemplation form in us the mind and heart of Christ.

I do not think we can overemphasize or be too conscious of that basic Christian tenet of the Presence. Whether we think of it in biblical terms of indwelling or the more theological concepts of immanence or the divine creative energies present and active in us.

You can undoubtedly recall that first day in the Lord's ministry. He had been baptized and then made his forty-day retreat in the desert. As he came forth the Baptizer pointed him out to his disciples: "Behold, the Lamb of God." And two eager young men went running after him. "What do you want?" The first recorded words of our Lord to his disciples are words well worth pondering. What do we reply? The disciple whom Jesus loved knew what he wanted: "Master, where do you dwell?" He wanted to be a disciple. He wanted to be with his chosen master. Jesus did not really answer John on this occasion. He promised an eventual answer. It was at the Last Supper where John got his answer: "The Father and I will dwell in you." I like a warmer translation of that, richer in nuance: "The Father and I will make our home in you."

God does dwell in us, but not like a tenant in a rented apartment. At the Supper Jesus would go on to pray: "Father, may they be one in us, as you are in me and I am in you." The oneness of the Father and the Son is absolute; it is total. All that the Son does is the Father working in him, through him, with him, and vice versa. The Lord has said to us, "Without me, you can do nothing." Nothing! If we do anything, if we are to accomplish anything for our patients, it is the Lord working in us, through us, with us. All the energies we expend of mind and heart, of body and feeling, are the workings of the divine creative energies active within us.

The last time I was with Mother Teresa of Calcutta, after breakfast as I was about to take my leave, I asked Mother to give me a "word of life" for my brothers at home. Mother looked at me intently. I felt myself drawn into those deep, deep eyes and embraced with an unforgettable love. After a silence that was of heaven and had no earthly measure of time, Mother said to me very slowly with great emphasis, "Tell them . . . to pray . . . that I do not get in God's way."

I think this is a prayer we all want to make our own. God is present in us, living and intensely active, an immense Love that wants to convey itself to each one we come to. We do not want to get in the way of the communication of that love. "Blessed are the pure in heart, for they shall see God." But also, others shall see God in them, through them. God will make the Love that God is present to our patients with all the divine consolation and comfort, tenderness, and strength if we do not get in the way, if there is enough humility and simplicity to allow the experience of God that we have had in our lectio and contemplation to shine forth.

PHYSICAL APPEARANCE

Each of us has our own image of Christ. It may come from images we repeatedly saw in church or in our own home when we were little. Or it might have developed from later, powerfully moving presentations of Christ on TV, in the movies or in books, scholarly or fictional. If we close our eyes and think of Jesus, our imaginations quickly bring forth some image of our Savior. If this is true of us, it certainly is also true of the Christians we approach in ministry.

Coming to the patient as a Christ-person, seeking to make Christ truly present with his caring love and healing power, it is of course impossible for us to replicate the physical image that our patient has of the Lord. What is important is that we do come as the meek and humble Lord, who came not to be ministered unto but to minister. But it also is important that our physical image does not do violence to the patient's image of Christ. I do think it is a bit ridiculous to say that a woman cannot image Christ because he was a man. But I do think it is difficult for the patient to receive as the bearer of the Good News, a florid person who is grossly overweight and is obviously desecrating his or her own body. I do not think it is even necessary to mention the countersign of a slovenly, unkempt, or unclean appearance.

We do need to take care of ourselves and keep in good physical shape, in so far as it can be reasonably expected of us. We may well get more than enough exercise running up and down the corridors of the hospital. But this may not be the case. If our weight is not healthy—and we who work so close to the health professions should be very conscious of this—we need to check on this. The villain, however, might well be our diet. After a long, hard, draining day at the hospital, it is very easy to fall victim to the mesmerization of the TV, to snack food, to yet another beer or a nightcap or two, etc. Coffee breaks are danger spots, too, with all those goodies that surround the coffee pot. It is amazing how much junk food is readily available in health care facilities! Sleep, too, is important. We can look really hung over if we are sleep-deprived.

Charity begins at home. We are to love our neighbor as we love ourselves. As one of my brethren once chided me, if you burn the candle at both ends you end up with a big drip. Christ-persons do not work tirelessly. They tire just like their Master. And they know, like him, when it is time to sit and rest, to go apart and rest for a while. They keep a coterie of devoted fellow workers and accept their care and concern. The humility to appropriately let go and let God is an important virtue: "Learn of me, for I am meek and humble of heart." Caring for ourselves is caring for Christ and enables us with Christ to care for others.

I am happy to be able to say that my own experiences as a patient have been few and far between. But as I think over them one figure stands out among all those who ministered to me. I was in a hospital under the care of the Daughters of Charity, and they had a beautiful practice in this hospital. To each floor was assigned one or two elderly sisters. Their years of nursing or administrating were behind them. Their ministry now was simply to move along the floor, visiting each of the patients. They were such a beautiful, serene, comforting presence. They did not say much; they smiled more. They listened. They prayed. They moved in and out, leaving peace behind them. Theirs was, indeed, simply and wholly a ministry of presence, and I must say the image of Sister Oliva and Sister Basila ministered to me to this day. Blessed are the chaplains, who are harried about many things, whose ministry is backed up with such assistance. But I am confident that chaplains who must be solicitous about many things can yet be such a presence if they but be good to themselves, care for themselves with the tender care they would bring to their dearest, the care they would counsel others to practice.

Chapter 5

The Power of Sacrament

I was assigned to a monastery on the island of Lantao for eight years, helping the community prepare for their integration into the Peoples Republic of China. With some frequency I would fly home to my monastery in Massachusetts. As we winged our way over the Pacific we were fed three movies and a couple of meals. I remember one particular movie—you probably saw it. It was the story of an eminent physician who taught at a university medical school. Unexpectedly one day he was diagnosed with throat cancer and he found himself on the other side of the desk. It was quite a learning experience for him. When he was finally able to resume his teaching post the first thing he did was have his class don those immodest little johnnies that strip patients of any outward sign of their dignity and then undergo the usual admission process plus some placebo tests, enema, and bed pan. I think that those of us who have been "on the other side of the desk," who have spent our days in a hospital bed, have a better chance of being truly compassionate chaplains. We know a little bit more about the "wounded healer."

A few years ago I was in a small county hospital for knee surgery. It was a rather affluent county so the hospital was very well equipped and staffed. In all there were twenty-seven assigned chaplains! Most mornings and afternoons I would be blessed with the visit of one or two of them. The local Catholic pastor brought the holy oils for anointing. A Eucharistic minister brought the

The Christ Chaplain
© 2007 by The Haworth Press, Inc. All rights reserved.
doi:10.1300/5931_06

Bread of Life each day. The others brought the Word of Life and their own wonderful presence.

Some of our Christian churches have a very well-developed sacramental theology and a very precise sacramental system. Others think less in this direction. But every Christian ministry is sacramental. Christ is the great sacrament of God's caring love for each of us. The Church itself is a caring and loving community that bespeaks the community toward which we grow in the Kingdom. Every word is a sacrament or symbol but when that Word is divinely inspired it is a sacrament with a blessing and richness beyond what we can ever hope to fully grasp.

Our Orthodox sisters and brothers have perhaps the fullest sacramental tradition. I recently attended the baptism of the daughter of my dentist. The little one was fully immersed three times in the saving waters (the font was equipped with hot and cold faucets and mother duly tested the water before the immersions) and then placed in the godparents' outstretched hands, which were full of holy oil. The little one was oiled from top to toe and anointed with sweet-smelling chrism by the pastor. Then, clothed in shining white garments that caught the dancing light of the illuminating candle, sucking on a thumb that had been dipped in the sacred chalice, this new Christian was allowed to taste and see how sweet is the Lord.

I would not presume to affirm how much this sacramental experience affected on the little recipient, though I suspect psychologists would have something to say about it. But I do know that we who were privileged to share this sacramental moment with the child were deeply affected by the fullness of the sacramental signs. That child was certainly washed in the waters of baptism. The oil of grace touched and strengthened the child wholly. The newness of life in Christ radiated in the beautiful white garment; the light was warmly shared with us in the burning candle. When the child received the food of life from the same chalice we ourselves had shared, we knew that this newly baptized was one with us in communion with Christ our Savior. The meaning, the reality, was conveyed to us in the words the priest spoke, but far more effectively in the sacramental actions we saw, smelled, and touched. When a patient's receptive faculties are diminishing through disease or age it would seem all the more important to employ the richness of sacramental sign to bring our message of love and care through as many faculties as possible. They amplify the important and basic message of our presence.

Standing by the bed of a fearful, hurting, lonely patient, I have often wished I could roll up my sleeves and with strengthening and comforting oil massage the whole body of this dear one, letting him experience the fuller consolation and encouragement of loving and compassionate touch. Sometimes words do not seem to be enough.

THE BIBLE

The Bible is a wonderful sacrament, an outward sign of an inner reality, a book that bespeaks a Divine Presence and enables the Divine to speak. The book we use and the way we use it can support, augment, or deflect the power of the Word. It is a book that is held with reverence, that is obviously cared for, yet not less obviously well used. We keep it ready at hand and use it to bring the Lord appropriately into the conversation. "Where two or three are gathered in my name, there I am in the midst." The Lord is with us; we want to let him have his chance to speak. He has given us his Word; it is for us to give it voice.

WATER

While the Eucharist, the sacrament of bread and wine, is the supreme sacrament Christ gives us, a sacred meal that nourishes the divine life within us, baptism is the more universal and basic sacrament. We hear the Lord's parting words: "Go forth and baptize all." I wish, as we might quite legitimately do, we would more commonly translate the text: "Go forth and wash all." A sacramental washing can help us to experience the cleaning we most deeply desire and need, a cleansing from the sin, the guilt, the evil, the dirt, the stain, the depravity that plagues our deepest being and deprives us of the peace and the experience of God's love that we need so much. Call it what you will—listen to what the patient calls it, that from which the patient senses a need to be freed.

The administration of the formal sacrament of baptism may not often be appropriate. Most Christians hold it to be a once in a lifetime event. But we can still use water—an anointing, a gentle pouring, a sprinkling, or in a soothing cloth, applied to the forehead or hands—to convey to the repentant patient that God's forgiveness is theirs, that all their sin and stain are wiped away, that a prodigal Father joyfully welcomes them with a loving, healing embrace. As we say "Mary/John/Joe, the Lord forgives you all your sins and washes away all the memory of them, all the stain they may have left," if we gently wipe the face or hands with a damp soothing cloth, the message is more apt to reach the depths where it needs to be heard and experienced if it is going to bring the peace that the patient longs for and needs. When touch is not possible, a significant sprinkling may help. We all want to be washed clean.

ANOINTING WITH OIL

This passage from the Epistle of Saint James, the brother of the Lord, is familiar:

Any of you who are ill should send for the elders of the church and they must anoint you with oil in the name of the Lord and pray over you. The prayer of faith will save you and the Lord will raise you up again; and if you have committed any sins, you will be forgiven.

Some churches have authoritatively given this anointing sacramental status. A Catholic priest, coming to the hospital, will almost always have blessed oil with him and know the ritual words by heart. He must take care not to succumb to rote and anoint in a way that downgrades the anoiting's natural sacramental power. Every Christian can use oil in a sacramental way. Oil of its very nature bespeaks vitality and strengthening, soothing and comforting. Those who have been athletes may have a more profound sense of this. To have oil applied in a meaningful way, with prayer, speaks to the patient in many ways: the caring touch, the sweet odor, the lingering presence. It can reinforce words or completely supply for them, reaching places where words can no longer penetrate or never could.

BREAD AND WINE

Jesus chose bread and wine as the great sacrament in his community. Usually it is not easy to bring off a sacramental meal in the context of a hospital room, though it certainly has often enough been done to the great consolation of patient and family. However the Bread of Life brought from the community table at home can speak of more than the nourishing presence of the Lord. It can convey an abiding unity with the community that can be comforting and strengthening. The many remain one in the one Bread. Other sharings of food or flowers or other appropriate messengers can also serve to bring this gift.

GESTURES

Almost without forethought, though some forethought could be fruitful, we use various gestures to help us express our prayer thoughts. We trace the air or a forehead or our own bodies with the sign of the cross. We gently and lovingly impose a hand on head or wounded part. We close our eyes or raise them to heaven—as Jesus so often did—or fold our hands or extend them in prayer. The frescoes in the catacombs of the *orantes* come to mind here. Gestures augment the communication of our presence and message, inviting the senses of sight and touch to come into play.

THE CHAPLAIN

Perhaps the most important and effective sacrament is the person of the chaplain. In their coming, chaplains express Christ's interest and love for the patient. Admiration and praise can be important here. We all need to feel we have some importance, especially when we are facing some dire diminishment. Certainly we know that every patient is important to Christ. That is why we are there. We can, though, take this so much for granted that we do not realize the need the patient has for us to express this, and to express it sincerely, an expression that comes out of our immediate experience of this particular patient. This comes from a mindfulness that becomes spontaneous only through the development of a contemplative attitude toward life, an attitude that is sensitive to the divine presence and beauty in all that is. Such an attitude comes with an almost worshipful reverence that invites patients to be aware of their own dignity, of their own goodness, worth, and beauty. With such a sense of self the patient can open more readily to the Divine Love, can accept the invitation to an intimate trusting friendship. When the brother or sister who comes is obviously happy in such a friendship, when they speak gently and tenderly of such a friendship, they can be readily heard. We want to be the sacrament, the outward sign of all that we say.

Chapter 6

Sharing the Word

Rather spontaneously, I think we have all said at one time or another, "Lord, teach me how to pray." In their youth many Catholics would have asked Mary, the Mother of Jesus:

> Lovely Lady, dressed in blue,
>   teach me how to pray.
> God was but your little boy
>   and you know the way.

It is in and through the Scriptures that the Lord teaches us how to pray.

Most of those to whom we minister would be quick to tell us that they have never learned any of the Scriptures by heart. Yet if we ask them, "Do you pray the Lord's Prayer?" they would even more quickly assure us that they do. That, of course, is Scripture. And, in fact, there would probably be in their repertoire many other scriptural prayers, such as the one with which we opened this chapter "Lord, teach us how to pray." The opening words of Psalm 69 are well known: "O God, come to my assistance. O Lord, make haste to help me." Words come to us from Gethsemane: "Not my will but thine be done." And from Calvary: "Father, into your hands I commend my spirit." Even, "I thirst," which was a favorite prayer of Mother Theresa of Calcutta.

The Christ Chaplain
© 2007 by The Haworth Press, Inc. All rights reserved.
doi:10.1300/5931_07

43

Throughout the Scriptures the Lord does teach us how to pray. Even more, he inaugurates a conversation with us. If lectio is listening, hearing, then it automatically leads to *oratio,* prayer, responding. When we really hear someone, we respond, even if it is only to shake our head, literally or metaphorically, in agreement or disagreement. The important thing is to get hold of the insight of lectio. It is very simply this: The Lord is in his inspired word. He speaks to us through and with that word. When we come to lectio we wisely let him get in the first word. We listen and we respond. We learn how to respond. Our minds and our hearts are formed by the Lord's saving word.

Learning that the Lord is in his word and speaks to us through his word is a wonderful gift for anyone and for everyone, but especially for those who are lonely, who feel abandoned and alone, or who have hours to lie in bed or sit in a chair with nothing whatsoever demanding their time or attention. What a blessing to be able to open a Bible and experience the Lord's presence and enter a loving converse with the Lord.

There was a time when every bed stand in hospitals, just as in hotels, was supplied with a Bible. For several good reasons that is no longer the case. It is part of our ministry to bring to those to whom we minister, in one way or another, the saving and comforting Word as well as the insight which will enable them to perceive that loving Presence and enjoy and profit from it.

We might well come armed with the Scriptures. The American Bible Society has wonderful little booklets with each of the Gospels that cost but a few cents, and they have large-print texts, which are oftentimes what is needed. Our budget might cover a steady supply of these, or we might need to divert some of the alms we would send to Food for the Poor or the like in order to be able to respond to the hunger of those to whom we are ministering. Or we might make our own booklets by photocopying a few pages of selected scriptural prayers in large print.

Ministry, of course, always has to be adapted completely to the ones to whom we are ministering. The potential receptivity of the patient may be greatly diminished by many factors. At times we find ourselves ministering more to the loved ones gathered around the bed than to the patient in the bed, and there are many diminishing factors among them also. The ministry may have to be the simplest, a tiny seed sown that we water with our ongoing prayer in the hope that the Lord may deign to grant an increase unto life eternal.

Where there is the time and openness, we can usually best share the gift of *lectio* by modeling it. At an appropriate moment in our encounter we might say, as we open our Bible, "When I was listening to the Lord this morning, he said this [text], and hearing this, I thought and I said to him. . . ."

Of course, we can do this authentically only if lectio has been a part of our journey, if we have been listening and responding to the Lord. I am still somewhat amazed, even though it has been a continuous experience over the years, how often the message I have received from the Lord on a particular morning proves to be just what some of those to whom I minister that day need to hear. Without that Word which I received that morning I would hardly have been able to respond to the need that was being laid out before me. The Lord provides, gently, powerfully, most fruitfully.

We will have patients whose ability to read will be inhibited temporarily or permanently. It is good to be aware of what might be available on TV or radio locally in regard to Scripture readings and commentary. Still, timely guidance as to how to receive the Word in the mode of lectio can be a real blessing. Otherwise, words are apt to go in one ear and out the other, so to speak. To encourage that kind of meditation *(meditatio)* we discussed previously can be helpful here. To catch a word, phrase, or sentence and hang on to it can open the way for the heard Word to abide with deepening insight and comfort.

One day a very elderly nun approached Saint Teresa of Avila, who was undoubtedly one of the great mystics of her time. The old nun asked her, "Mother, how can I become a contemplative?" Mother Teresa's reply was the simplest and perfectly adapted to the dear old woman: "Sister, pray the 'Our Father' but take an hour to pray it." The Saint was inviting the old nun to enter *lectio,* meditation, and pray in a way that could quickly open out into contemplation. In all likelihood, the nun could not read. And even if she could read, she probably would not have ready access to a Bible; printing was just getting under way. But almost certainly she would know the particular passage from the Sermon on the Mount which we call the Lord's Prayer. Taking her time, she could again hear the Lord speak these words, speak to her. She could make them her own, speak them back to him. She could enter them and let them open out, revealing little by little the inexhaustible riches they contain and seek to express. As they opened out, they would call forth an ever deeper response from the heart of Sister until finally they led her into the deepest of responses, the silence that is contemplation.

Most Christians we minister to will have some words of sacred Scripture written in the book of their memory, probably the Lord's Prayer and other favorite sayings of the Lord. If their condition does not allow them to take a Bible in hand, they can turn to that inner book, gather a favored phrase, let it be present, and like Mary, ponder it in the heart. Even if particular words are lacking, scenes can be evoked. After the shepherds' visit to the stable in Bethlehem, Saint Luke tells us that Mary "pondered all these things in her heart." A return to the stable, which for many brings forth warm, happy, comforting memories, might be a good place for a restless, pained patient to find some rest. The Scriptures first speak to us in pictures. This was true for the Church as a whole with the frescoes in the catacombs, the mosaics, the icons, the stained glass, the paintings of the masters and of lesser artists. And it was true for many of us in picture books and coloring books and those windows in church where the light of the Gospels shines forth. The whole of the Bible can be read in that twelfth-century "comic book," the windows of the Cathedral of Chartres. With a little listening we can perhaps discern what scene from the Bible it might be most helpful for a particular patient to call up.

A WORD OF LIFE

In the early Church, and even today among our Orthodox brothers and sisters, a spiritual seeker turns to a spiritual father or mother, asking for "A Word of Life." A favorite one—a rather long one drawn from two separate Gospel stories—has been "Lord Jesus Christ, Son of the living God, have mercy on me a sinner." In practice it is usually rather quickly simplified, according to the disciples' present state. "Lord, be merciful to me a sinner," or "Lord Jesus, Son of God!" Benedict of Nursia, in the climax of his *Rule for Monasteries,* exclaims, "What page, what passage of the Old and New Testaments is not the truest of guides for human life!" Chaplains, even if they hesitate to think of themselves as spiritual mothers or fathers can still when it seems appropriate, give a patient a Word of Life that can abide with the patient and bring light and peace and comfort. For one reason or another, a word may be all that one can give and yet it may be enough as the Lord deigns to use it as an immense channel of grace.

Where there is the time and openness, we may be able to share the method of lectio more fully with our patient. It is important to always keep it simple. And it is most helpful if there is time to actually do a bit of lectio together, listening, sharing what we hear and the response to what it is calling forth. A simple sheet or folder describing the method could be left with the patient. Giving a patient the gift of lectio and the means to enjoy it opens a very effective way for the Lord to continue his visit, his ministry after we have to move on.

Chapter 7

Resting in the Presence

Jim and I were born the same day. We lived in neighboring towns. When it came time for high school we found ourselves classmates. The bond grew with the years. I remember well the day I visited his mother in the hospital. We chatted for a while. "Mom" was always interested in everything "her boys" were doing. After a bit, though, Mom said very plaintively: "I can't pray. I lie here all day but I just can't seem to pray like I do at home." I pulled my chair closer to the bed and said: "Let's try something." I reached out and took her hand gently in mine, and said: "Now, just close your eyes. Jesus is present in your heart, dwelling there, loving you, caring for you. Tell him how much you love him. How much you want to pray." We were quiet for a bit. Then I said: "Now just repeat his name lovingly. Jesus . . . Jesus . . . Jesus." We continued in silence. Twenty minutes later, I gently began to pray the Lord's Prayer, phrase by phrase, savoring each phrase.

That was the day Mom learned centering prayer. When I finished the Lord's Prayer I gave her hand a little squeeze. She opened her eyes, a broad, peaceful smile blossoming. I did not have to ask about her prayer. The fruit was self-evident. I left with Mom one of the folders from Food for the Poor. Happily, Mom began to make a strong recovery and I was soon able to visit her at home. Without making any claims I can say this: the deep rest one finds in centering must surely be an aid to recovery. The important

The Christ Chaplain
© 2007 by The Haworth Press, Inc. All rights reserved.
doi:10.1300/5931_08

thing here was that Mom now could pray and gratefully spent a good bit of her remaining time in the hospital in centering prayer.

Another memory comes quickly to me now. This was years later. I was traveling widely by this time, sharing centering prayer in many places. This particular evening I had just flown to a southern city. I was to lead a day on lectio and centering prayer the next day. The priest who met me took me to a convent near the airport to have supper with the parish team there. Of course, there were all sorts of questions about what I was doing. When I described centering prayer I was asked: "Couldn't you give us a mini-course as soon as we finish the dishes?"

So we gathered in the community room. Very quickly I went through the basics: getting settled, posture, closing the eyes, then the three points of the method and the Lord's Prayer. Then we enjoyed together twenty minutes of centering. (As a rule, I never allow folks to ask questions before praying, otherwise we can find ourselves struggling with a lot of theoretic questions. After the prayer, we can look at the real questions, coming out of experience.) As the leader I began with a very brief vocal prayer, expressing our faith and love: "Lord, we believe you are truly here present within us. For these few minutes we want to give ourselves completely to you in love." At the end of the twenty minutes I gently gave voice to the Lord's Prayer, phrase by phrase. As I opened my eyes I looked about. I saw a wonderful radiant smile on the face of Sister Penelope.

"You must have had a beautiful experience, Pen."

"Yes," she said, "That was the first time in weeks that I have been able to forget my pain." Sister was living with terminal bone cancer.

About six months later, when I came back to that city to do a follow-up, I was taken to visit Sister Penelope in the hospital. The end was near. Though her face was drained and tired, a sparkling joy shown in her eyes. She was enthusiastic in her expressions of gratitude for centering prayer: "Thanks to it, these past months have been a beginning of heaven on earth." As her physical abilities ebbed and her pain increased, Sister had been spending more and more time at the center. And the Lord, her consoler, her comforter, her life, her love was there with her.

Saint Paul tells us that the fruits of the Spirit are love, joy, peace, patience. Their presence is not always so richly experienced. More often perhaps it is a question of a subtle, gentle interior growth over time. But the Lord can be very lavish in his gifts. For most of us, most of the time, centering prayer is a prayer in faith. But when the need is special, the Lord can make his presence felt in a special way. Centering prayer gives him a chance to do that. It is a way to open the door. "Behold, I stand at the door and knock. And if one opens, I will come in and sit down side by side with that one and we will sup together." The Lord longs to be with us. And intimately: we are to sit, not across the table, but side by side, up close, as close as we want. But there is that "if": "If one opens . . ." He never forces his way in.

Have you ever heard the story of that mosaic in Satin Peter's Basilica in Rome? It depicts Jesus knocking at the door. It was done by one of the most famous artists of the time. The day it was unveiled quite a crowd was present, including the pope himself. As the veil dropped, all eyes eagerly studied the new creation. Then a murmuring arose among the bright young students. They had spotted that the door had no latch. The master had missed it. The criticism was made to the master. "Oh no," he replied. "It was not forgotten. This door only opens from the inside."

Our ministry can show folks how to gently open that door so that the Master can come in.

How often are our patients men or women of action, real doers. They are not good patients because they can hardly be patient. When they find themselves lying there, unable to do anything, they feel exceedingly frustrated, very restless. They want to be doing something. They want to continue to make a difference. We might minister to such patients by offering them some theological insight.

I believe one of the great spiritual masters of the last century was the Jesuit paleontologist, Pierre Teilhard de Chardin. Many of his works have been translated into English. Nonetheless he is still difficult to read. His friend, Henri de Lubac can perhaps help us understand him. Teilhard de Chardin had an amazing grasp of the unity of all being. When our beneficent Creator said his "Let there be . . ." and primal matter, packed with Divine Creative Energy, came into being, the stage was set for science's basic hypothesis of the so-called "Big Bang" and evolution began. A power and design far beyond what our human minds have yet been able to grasp began to move the creation toward its consummation in the Omega, in Christ, in deification, as our Orthodox sisters and brothers would say. "All things are yours, and you are Christ's and Christ is God's" is the way Paul put it. Each of us in everything we do has the potency to move the creative process forward and upward, toward its full realization.

Our Lord expressed all this so much more simply, as was his wont, in the parable of the leaven. If we have ever made bread, his image speaks so much more powerfully to us. Just a few little grains, hardly a teaspoonful of yeast, buried under a whole pile of dampened flour, begins to do its work. Soon the whole mass of dough rises. We beat it down, and it rises again. We beat it down again, and it rises again. The energy within the leaven seems to be ceaseless, and in a sense it is. For a bit of leavened dough kept for the next day can begin the whole process again.

What is the leaven of creation that drives it forward and causes it to rise? God is love. And it is his love, above all in us, that moves the evolution forward and causes it to rise to an ever greater humanization and ultimately to deification. The human connection alone would postulate our interconnection and mutual edification. But with the fuller revelation in Christ and our union within him, this becomes so much more cogent. Each one of us can be a powerful leaven of love, hidden deep within, lifting up the whole. We may be but one in six billion here on earth at this moment, but we can make a difference. Perhaps our restless doers can find some rest if they can realize that just by resting there in the divine love at the center of their being, they can perhaps be doing more than they ever did before to make this world a better place in which to live, can move the human community toward being a community of love.

Another word of the Lord might speak more effectively to some. The restless ones have often been "Martha's," busy about many things, busy doing things for the Lord himself. Now maybe they can hear the Lord: "Martha, Martha, you are busy about many things. But only one thing is necessary. Mary has chosen the best part." Yes, the Greek text does not make the comparison of "the better part," but states absolutely, "the best part." Mary sits there, wide open, receiving the full outpouring of divine love from Christ. Saint Bernard of Clairvaux reminds us that she was not a pipe, with the love just passing through. She was a reservoir, receiving the love in fullness, until it overflows and pours out upon all in the house, in the community, in the world. The patient's simple, intensely active receptivity, totally open to the divine love, can be one of the reservoirs that can water a tormented, strife-riven world parched for the waters of love. Our downtime can be exceedingly productive and meaningful and the realization of this new way of making a difference immensely comforting to the active doer.

Chapter 8

A Final Word

In our monastery on Lantao Island we had a wonderful old monk, Father Justin McCabe. Father had served in Quailing, China, until he was arrested in 1950. After two years of harrowing imprisonment he was expelled and continued his missionary work on Taiwan. When he was seventy-two and told he had to retire back to the United States, he choose rather to join the monastic community on Lantao Island, for he wanted to die and be buried in China. He celebrated his eighy-eighth birthday by placing on his door a banner: "Today is the first day of the rest of my life."

There are times when the work of "now" is the past, during a retreat or with a psychologist or counselor, to look at our foundations and perhaps do some repair. But we do not want today to be filled with the past; rather we want to look to the future.

We have a tendency to create the future out of the past, to make the future only more of the past. It is extremely limiting to live out of the limitations of the past. Nonetheless we tend to do this for the sake of some imagined security. "I survived the past. If I create a future like it, then I know I can survive." The "troubles," as they speak of them in North Ireland, go on and on because the future is constantly envisioned out of the past. And so too in Israel, in many other places, and in most of our personal lives.

If you have created such a future for yourself, I would invite you to take it gently and set it to one side. I do not want to take it away from you. But set it aside to give yourself some freedom and

The Christ Chaplain
© 2007 by The Haworth Press, Inc. All rights reserved.
doi:10.1300/5931_09

space. Now, in this space totally unencumbered, create a vision of the future, the future you really want. Create a vision of the life you would really like to live. Create a vision of your family, of your hospital as you never before thought possible because you were wearing the blinders of the past. Let us take off the blinders and let the whole realm of possibility in. It is a magnificent world, the creation of a magnificent God, who plans a new heaven and a new earth.

There was an extraordinary paleontologist who lived in the first half of the past century. I have already mentioned him—Father Pierre Teilhard de Chardin. He was a man of hope, a man who always lived into the future, a magnificent future. He loved the "phenomenon of man" and saw all as it truly is, a "divine milieu." He was a stretcher-bearer on the front line in World War I. He was in China when the nuclear age opened with the horror of Hiroshima and Nagasaki. Yet he never lost his enthusiastic faith—no matter how much superiors and colleagues of less visionary faith sought to put him down and silence him. The whole of the creation from the "big bang" till today and on is moving unfalteringly, no matter how much we falter, toward the "Omega Point," toward the total fullness of all in Christ Jesus, the true God who is true man, one with us in our humanity. Teilhard caught Saint Paul's vision:

> In him all created things took their being, heavenly and earthly, visible and invisible. . . . They were all created through him and in him; he takes precedence of all, and in him all subsist. . . . It was God's good pleasure to let all completeness dwell in him, and through him to win back all things, whether on earth or in heaven, unto union with himself; making peace with them through his blood, shed on the cross. (Colossians 1:16-20)

And he made it his own.

What is our vision? Is it big enough, sufficiently worthy of who we are, to fill each day with the deep excitement of hope? Hope is a fundamental virtue of a people who believe in a Risen Christ, in the resurrection of the body and life everlasting. Perhaps this is the thing we most need to bring into the hospital room, into all our ministry, a love that expresses itself in an absolutely indemonstrable hope. I know in whom I believe. I know him because I have spent time with him day after day in lectio. I know him because we have shared intimacy at the Center. I know him and I know that in him the victory is ultimately ours.

Appendix

Selected Readings

FINDING PEACE AT THE CENTER*

In this brochure we discuss two simple, traditional methods of being to the Lord as the Source of our peace: Scriptural prayer or Sacred Listening and Contemplative or Centering Prayer. Take some time every day for one or both of these prayer methods, and allow God to be to you the Source of Love, Life, Peace and Happiness that He wants to be.

"Peace!"—"Shalom!"—"Peace be with you!" This was the first greeting of the Risen Lord. And it is the heartfelt need and desire of everey human person. It is the great concern of our times. But there can be no peace in this world of ours, no peace among nations, unless there is first peace in our own hearts. Only then can we be instruments of Christ's peace, doing the works of justice and love that lead to peace.

The Way to Peace

How do we find peace? How do we come to possess inner peace so that we can bring peace to others?

---

*Reprinted with permission by Food for the Poor.

The Christ Chaplain
© 2007 by The Haworth Press, Inc. All rights reserved.
doi:10.1300/5931_10

On the night before he died, he who is the Way and the Truth and the Life, our Lord Jesus, gathered his most intimate friends for a final meal. There he poured out his heart to them, sharing with them the deepest secrets of his love. He told them—and us: "The one who loves me keeps my word"—we hold fast to all that he tells us and make it the foundation of our lives: "The just person lives by faith." "The one who loves me keeps my word and my Father and I come and dwell in that one. . . . My word is not my own, it is the word of the one who sent me. The Advocate, Holy Spirit, whom the Father will send in my name will teach you everything and remind you of all that I have said to you. Peace I bequeath to you, my own peace I give you, a peace the world cannot give, this is my gift to you." The Father, Son, and Holy Spirit have come and taken up their abode in us to bring to us their own peace, that peace that comes from knowing how much we are loved and cared for by the One who has care of all the world, the Almighty, the All-loving.

The way to a deep inner peace is to be in touch with this inner reality. Too often our prayer is one of words, thoughts, images, concepts—all things produced by our mind. No wonder we often find prayer tiresome, hardly refreshing. Yet, Jesus has said: "Come to me all you who labor and are heavily burdened, and I will refresh you." Prayer should be refreshing. We need to learn to listen, to listen with love, to listen in love.

Sacred Reading—or Listening

The place we can most easily hear the Lord is in the Scriptures.

The Bible should be among our most precious possessions. It should never be simply left lying about or shelved among the other books. Rather, it should be enthroned in our homes and offices as a Real Presence of the Lord in our midst.

Each day we want to take a few minutes to listen to the Lord speaking to us in his inspired Word. We take our Bible with great reverence, aware of his Presence. We kiss the Bible and ask the Holy Spirit who inspired the writer and who lives in us to make the Word come alive now in us. Then, we listen for a few minutes. We respond as we are moved. If the Lord speaks powerfully to us, we simply abide in his word and presence. At the end of our time, we thank the Lord (Isn't it wonderful we can have him speak to us whenever we want!); and, we take away from our encounter a thought or word to carry with us through the day.

A Deeper Listening

At that same Last Supper, Jesus told his disciples—all of us: I no longer call you servants, but *friends,* because I make known to you all that the Father has made known to me—all the secrets of my heart. We have been made for a deep intimate friendship with the Lord. Our hearts long for it. As a great sinner who became a great saint once cried: "Our hearts are made for you, O Lord, and they will not rest until they rest in you!" We are not content with just listening to the Lord's words, no matter how wonderful they are. We want a deeper, more experiential union with him. It is like any true friendship: as it grows it needs to go beyond words and doing things together and for each other. *The image* God himself has frequently used is that of the marital embrace, that total being to each other. We need those times of prayer when we listen not just with our ears, our eyes, our minds, but more with our hearts, with our whole being.

This kind of prayer has sometimes been called contemplative prayer or prayer of the heart. It is a prayer of being. The tradition has passed down to us a simple way of entering into this kind of prayer. This traditional way is called today, Centering Prayer.

Centering Prayer

Centering prayer is a very simple way of prayer which can be used by anyone who wants to be with God, to experience his love and presence. It is a prayer of longing that leads into a prayer of Presence.

First of all, we settle ourselves down quietly. Most of us pray best sitting down, but take any posture that works well for you. It is best if the back is fairly straight and well supported. If we gently close our eyes, we immediately begin to quiet down, for we use a lot of our psychic energy in seeing.

Once we are settled, we turn our attention to the Lord present within is. We know he is there by faith, that is, we know he is there because he said so. In love, we turn ourselves over to him. For these twenty minutes, we are all his. He can do with us whatever he wants. This prayer is a pure gift, a gift of self in love.

In order to be able to abide quietly and attentively with our Beloved, we use a love word, a prayer word—a simple word that expresses our being to the Lord in love. It might well be our favorite name for him: Lord, Jesus, Father, Love—whatever is meaningful for us. We just let that word be there, to keep us attentive to him. It is not an effortful proclamation or a constantly repeated *mantra,* but rather a sigh of love, a murmur of love, a "being to."

Whenever, during the time of our prayer, we become aware of anything else, we simply use our love word to return to the Lord. Some days we will have to use the word constantly, there may be a lot of commotion around us or in us. No matter. Each time we use it, each time we return to him, it is a perfect gift of self to him in love. Other days we may not need to use our word much at all. Fine! It really makes no difference. Simply, these twenty minutes are all his to do with as he likes. We don't seek anything for ourselves. It is pure gift. It is not in the twenty minutes we will be aware of things. All our attention is on him. It is outside the time of prayer that we will begin to see the difference, as the fruits of the Spirit—love, peace, joy, kindness—begin to flourish in our lives.

At the end of our twenty minutes, we do not want to jump right back into activity. We have gone very deep even if we don't seem to sense it. So, we want to end our prayer very gently. I suggest praying interiorly, very slowly, the Our Father. Let each phrase come forth with all its meaning. In this, the Lord will teach us much. And the deep peace of our contemplative prayer will flow into our active lives.

It is a prayer of experience, so we can only know it by experience. We always urge people learning this prayer to make a commitment to themselves to practice the prayer faithfully, twice a day, for thirty days. Then, perhaps with a close friend, for someone else can usually see better than we, look and see what has been the fruit of the prayer in our lives. If the way we were praying before was producing better fruit, don't hesitate to return to it. But if this simple prayer of listening, attentive love has been good for us, then by all means continue in it. The important thing is that we do pray regularly and allow God to be to us the source of love, life, peace and happiness that he wants to be.

John the Baptist's father, Zechariah, tells us that Jesus came "to guide our feet into the way of peace." We have but to listen to the Lord—listen to him in his Word, listen to him in our hearts—and we shall find the peace we so long for, the peace that this world of ours so desperately needs. We will find that the peace already dwells in us at the center of our being, for there dwells the Prince of Peace, the Source of all peace.

LECTIO DIVINA: *SACRED READING*

It is well to keep the Sacred Scriptures enthroned in our home in a place of honor as a real Presence of the Word in our midst.

1. Take the Sacred Text with reverence and call upon the Holy Spirit.
2. For five minutes (or longer, if you are so drawn) listen to the Lord speaking to you through the Text, and respond to Him.
3. At the end of the time, choose a word or phrase (perhaps one will have been "given" to you) to take with you, and thank the Lord for being with you and speaking to you.

CENTERING PRAYER

Sit relaxed and quiet.

1. Be in faith and love to God who dwells in the center of your being.
2. Take up a love word and let it be gently present, supporting your being to God in faith-filled love.
3. Whenever you become aware of anything else, simply, gently return to the Lord with the use of your prayer word.

Let the Our Father (or some other prayer) pray itself.

A PRAYER FOR THE HOSPITAL

Our ministry, naturally enough, concerns itself first of all with the individual patient, then with the patient's family and visitors, and with the staff. But we live and work in a community and depend on that community to support and facilitate our ministry. It is true that the strength and vitality of a community comes from that of the individual members but it is also true that the strength and vitality of the community flows into all its members. Rightly then should the hospital or health care system have its place in our prayerful concern.

The chaplain's office of one hospital made this prayer available on a convenient prayer card to all those in ministry:

> Divine Creator, you have given us the mission of healing. Keep us all, in every corner of this hospital, focused on this mission as we face the challenging times of disease, trauma, and the demands of the contemporary workplace. It is too easy to move away from who we are and what we are to be doing. Bless all who administer and manage, all who provide direct care for patients, and all in the vital support services, as we seek to bring your blessing to all who come here for help. Let us always be about the healing work you have called us to do.

Suggested Further Readings

Casey, Michael. *Sacred Reading: The Ancient Art of Lectio Divina* (Liguori MO: Triumph Books, 1995).

De Lubac, Henri. *The Eternal Feminine: A Study on the Poem by Teilhard de Chardin* (New York: Harper & Row, 1971).

Hall, Thelma. *Too Deep for Words: Rediscovering Lectio Divina* (New York: Paulist, 1994).

Johnston, William (ed.). *The Cloud of Unknowing and the Book of Privy Counseling* (New York: Doubleday, 1973).

Keating, Thomas. *Active Meditations for Contemplative Prayer* (New York: Continuum, 1997).

_____. *Awakenings* (New York: Crossroad, 1990).

_____. *The Better Part: Stages of Contemplative Living* (New York: Continuum, 2000).

_____. *Foundations for Centering Prayer and the Christian Contemplative Life* (New York: Continuum, 2002).

_____. *The Heart of the World: An Introduction to Contemplative Christianity* (New York: Continuum, 1999).

_____. *The Human Condition: Contemplation and Transformation* (New York: Paulist Press, 1999).

_____. *Intimacy with God* (New York: Crossroad, 1994).

_____. *Invitation to Love: The Way of Christian Contemplation* (Rockport, MA: Element, 1992).

_____. *Journey to the Center: A Lenten Passage* (New York: Crossroad, 1999).

_____. *Open Mind, Open Heart: The Contemplative Dimension of the Gospel* (Rockport, MA: Element, 1992).

_____. *Reawakenings* (New York: Crossroad, 1992).

Lawrence, Brother. *The Practice of the Presence of God* (Springfield, IL: Templegate, 1974).

Meninger, William A. *The Loving Search for God: Contemplative Prayer and the Cloud of Unknowing* (New York: Continuum, 1994).

Merton, Thomas. *Contemplative Prayer* (New York: Doubleday, 1971).

_____. *Opening the Bible* (Collegeville, MI: The Liturgical Press, 1970).

Mulholland, Robert. *Shaped by the Word: The Power of Sacred Scripture in Spiritual Formation* (Nashville, TN: The Upper Room, 1985).

Muto, Susan. *A Practical Guide to Spiritual Reading* (Danville, NJ: Dimension Books, 1976).

Pennington, M. Basil. *Awake in the Spirit: A Personal Handbook on Prayer* (New York: Crossroad, 1992).

_____. *Call to the Center: The Gospel's Invitation to Deeper Prayer,* 3rd ed. (Hyde Park, NY: New City Press, 2003).

_____. *Centered Living: The Way of Centering Prayer* (Liguori, MO: Liguori, 1999).

_____. *Centering Prayer: Renewing an Ancient Christian Prayer Form* (Garden City, NY: Doubleday, 1980).

_____. *Daily We Touch Him: Practical Religious Experiences* (Kansas City: Sheed & Ward, 1997).

_____. *An Invitation to Centering Prayer* (Liguori, MO: Liguori, 2001).

_____. Lectio Divina: *Renewing the Ancient Practice of Praying the Scriptures* (New York: Crossroad, 1998).

_____. *Listening: God's Word for Today* (New York: Continuum, 2000).

_____. *Living in the Question: Meditations in the Style of Lectio Divina* (New York: Continuum, 1999).

_____. *Seeking His Mind: 40 Meetings with Christ* (Brewster, MA: Paraclete, 2002).

Pennington, M. Basil, Thomas Keating, and Thomas Clark. *Finding Grace at the Center: The Beginning of Centering Prayer* (Woodstock, VT: Skylight Paths, 2002).

Pollard, Miriam. *The Listening God* (Wilmington, DE: Michael Glazier, 1989).

Reininger, Gustave, ed. *Centering Prayer in Daily Life and Ministry* (New York: Continuum, 1998).

_____. *The Diversity of Centering Prayer* (New York: Continuum, 1999).

Richards, M. C. *Centering in Pottery, Poetry and the Person* (Middletown, CT: Wesleyan University Press, 1964).

Salvail, Ghislaine. *At the Crossroads of Scripture: An Introduction to Lectio Divina* (Boston, MA: Daughters of St. Paul, 1996).

Smith, Elizabeth, and Chalmers, Joseph. *A Deeper Love: An Introduction to Centering Prayer* (New York: Continuum, 1999).

Teilhard de Chardin, Pierre. *The Divine Milieu* (New York: Harper & Row, 1960).

_____. *The Phenomenon of Man* (New York: Harper Brothers, 1959).

Dear Customer:

Please fill out & return this form to receive special deals & publishing opportunities for you! These include:
- availability of new books in your local bookstore or online
- one-time prepublication discounts
- free or heavily discounted related titles
- free samples of related Haworth Press periodicals
- publishing opportunities in our periodicals or Book Division

❑ OK! Please keep me on your regular mailing list and/or e-mailing list for new announcements!

Name _____

Address_____

STAPLE OR TAPE YOUR BUSINESS CARD HERE!

_____

*E-mail address _____
*Your e-mail address will never be rented, shared, exchanged, sold, or divested. You may "opt-out" at any time. May we use your e-mail address for confirmations and other types of information? ❑ Yes ❑ No

Special needs:
Describe below any special information you would like:
- Forthcoming professional/textbooks
- New popular books
- Publishing opportunities in academic periodicals
- Free samples of periodicals in my area(s)

Special needs/Special areas of interest:

_____

_____

_____

_____

Please contact me as soon as possible. I have a special requirement/project:

_____

_____

_____

_____

The Haworth Press Inc.

PLEASE COMPLETE THE FORM ABOVE AND MAIL TO:
Donna Barnes, Marketing Dept., The Haworth Press, Inc.
10 Alice Street, Binghamton, NY 13904-1580 USA
Tel: 1-800-429-6784 • Outside US/Canada Tel: (607) 722-5857
Fax: 1-800-895-0582 • Outside US/Canada Fax: (607) 771-0012
E-mail: orders@HaworthPress.com

GBIC07

Visit our Web site: www.HaworthPress.com